YOU and ME

Poems of Friendship
selected and illustrated by
Salley Mavor

Orchard Books
New York

Orchard Books
95 Madison Avenue
New York, NY 10016

Manufactured in the United States of America
Printed by Barton Press, Inc.
Bound by Horowitz/Rae
Book design by Susan M. Sherman, Ars Agassiz, Cambridge, Massachusetts

10 9 8 7 6 5 4 3 2 1

Library of Congress Cataloging-in-Publication Data

You and me : poems of friendship / selected and illustrated by Salley Mavor.
    p. cm.
    Summary: A collection of poems about friendship, by such authors as
Jack Prelutsky, Langston Hughes, and Judith Viorst.
    ISBN 0-531-30045-5. — ISBN 0-531-33045-1 (lib. bdg.)
    1. Friendship — Juvenile poetry. 2. Children's poetry, American.
[1. Friendship — Poetry. 2. American poetry — Collections.]
I. Mavor, Salley.
PS595.F75Y68 1997
811.008'0354 — dc21   97-10062

to all my friends

A sidewalk is a wide walk
A let's-step-out-and-stride-walk
A two-abreast-let's-glide-walk
An arm-in-arm-let's-talk-walk
A pigeon-and-a-bug-walk
A shoulder-hugging-snug-walk
A hot-dog-and-balloon-walk
An under-sun-or-moon-walk
A grass-grows-in-the-crack-walk
A rainy-day-wet-track-walk
A place where you and I walk
And talk and talk and talk.

PATRICIA HUBBELL

Lemonade Stand

Every summer
under the shade
we fix up a stand
to sell lemonade.

A stack of cups,
a pitcher of ice,
a shirtboard sign
to tell the price.

A dime for the big,
A nickel for small.
The nickel cup's short.
The dime cup's tall.

Plenty of sugar
to make it sweet,
and sometimes cookies
for us to eat.

But when the sun
moves into the shade
it gets too hot
to sell lemonade.

Nobody stops
so we put things away
and drink what's left
and start to play.

MYRA COHN LIVINGSTON

5¢   10¢

Teresa's Red Adidas

(FOR T.G.)

I think that I shall never view
Shoes as nice as those on you.
They're red and soft with stripes of white.
One goes left, the other right.
I hope they let you run quick fast;
I also hope they last and last.
Shoes are made for feet like those,
And I just love the ones you chose.

PAUL B. JANECZKO

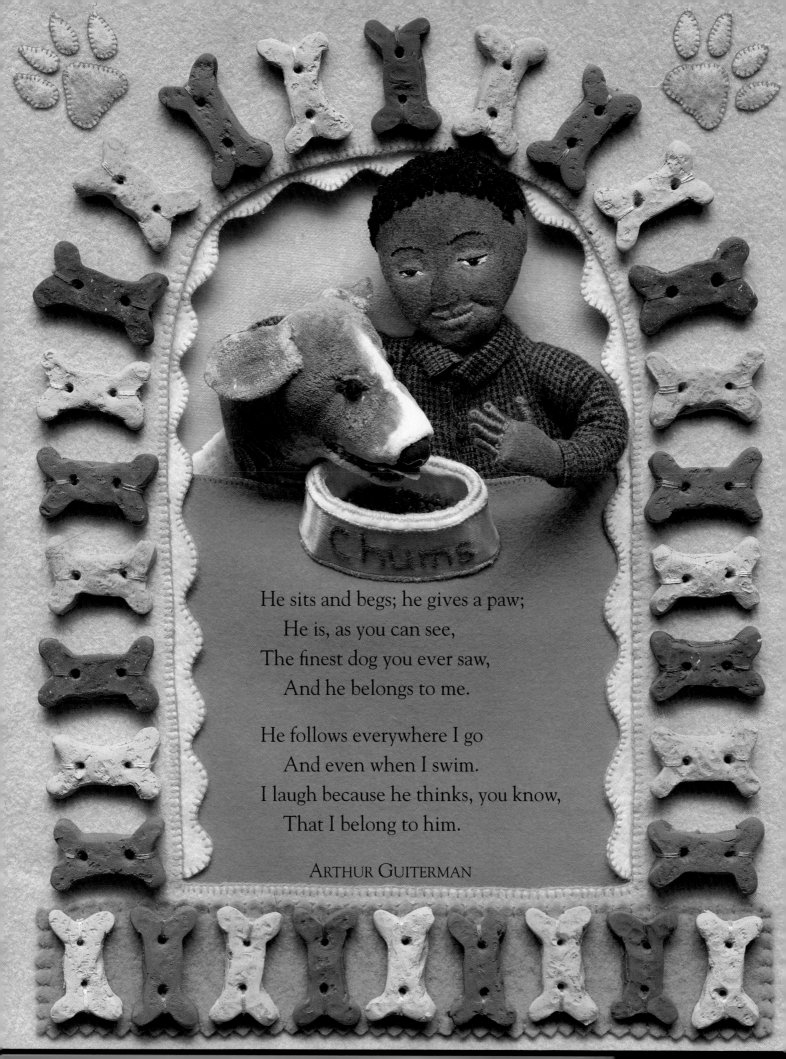

He sits and begs; he gives a paw;
  He is, as you can see,
The finest dog you ever saw,
  And he belongs to me.

He follows everywhere I go
  And even when I swim.
I laugh because he thinks, you know,
  That I belong to him.

ARTHUR GUITERMAN

I have a friend who keeps on standing on her hands.
That's fine,
Except I find it very difficult to talk to her
Unless I stand on mine.

KARLA KUSKIN

ROSE BURGUNDER

A Boy's Place

I know a place
that's oh, so green
where elephant ears
together lean;
a quiet place
that no one's seen
but me.

It's not very far
my secret spot.
I go whenever
the day's too hot
for friends or games
or a story's plot—
just me.

I leave my shoes
at home and go
over the wall
where the blackberries grow
and squoosh my toes
in the mud, with no
design.

A gentle jungle
of swamp and sky,
a curious bird
my only spy,
a place to whistle
each August by —
all mine!

My Natural Mama

my natural mama
is gingerbread
all brown and
spicy sweet.
some mamas are rye
or white or
golden wheat
but my natural mama
is gingerbread,
brown and spicy sweet.

LUCILLE CLIFTON

Hope

Sometimes when I'm lonely,
Don't know why,
Keep thinkin' I won't be lonely
By and by.

LANGSTON HUGHES

On Halloween

We mask our faces
and wear strange hats
and moan like witches
and screech like cats
and jump like goblins
and thump like elves
and almost manage
to scare *ourselves*.

AILEEN FISHER

Adoption

I found a kitten
     At the city pound,
A tiny creature
     My hands wrapped around.

I held it up
     Against my cheek
And I could feel
     Its wild heartbeat.

It touched me
     With its icy nose —
We liked each other
     From head to toes.

ISABEL JOSHLIN GLASER

PAT LOWERY COLLINS

How to Be a Friend

Keep a secret
Tell a wish
Listen
to
a dream

Fast Friends

MONICA KULLING

Ruth and me
take to the street
fast, then faster
pedaling feet.

Ruth and me
and our bikes in town,
slow up the hills
full speed coming down.

Ruth and me
it's easy to see—
my friend always
is what she'll be.

No Girls Allowed

When we're playing tag
and the girls want to play,
we yell and we scream
and we chase them away.

When we're playing stickball
or racing our toys
and the girls ask to join,
we say, "Only for boys."

We play hide-and-go-seek
and the girls wander near.
They say, "Please let us hide."
We pretend not to hear.

We don't care for girls
so we don't let them in,
we think that they're dumb—
and besides, they might win.

JACK PRELUTSKY

Since Hanna Moved Away

The tires on my bike are flat.
The sky is grouchy gray.
At least it sure feels like that
Since Hanna moved away.

Chocolate ice cream tastes like prunes.
December's come to stay.
They've taken back the Mays and Junes
Since Hanna moved away.

Flowers smell like halibut.
Velvet feels like hay.
Every handsome dog's a mutt
Since Hanna moved away.

Nothing's fun to laugh about.
Nothing's fun to play.
They call me, but I won't come out
Since Hanna moved away.

JUDITH VIORST

Two Friends

lydia and shirley have
two pierced ears and
two bare ones
five pigtails
two pairs of sneakers
two berets
two smiles
one necklace
one bracelet
lots of stripes and
one good friendship

NIKKI GIOVANNI

SNOW

We'll play in the snow
And stray in the snow
And stay in the snow
In a snow-white park.
We'll clown in the snow
And frown in the snow
Fall down in the snow
Till it's after dark.
We'll cook snow pies
In a big snow pan.
We'll make snow eyes
In a round snow man.

We'll sing snow songs
And chant snow chants
And roll in the snow
In our fat snow pants.
And when it's time to go home to eat
We'll have snow toes
On our frosted feet.

KARLA KUSKIN

BURSTING

We've laughed until my cheeks are tight.
We've laughed until my stomach's sore.
If we could only stop we might
Remember what we're laughing for.

DOROTHY ALDIS

Tumbling

In jumping and tumbling
   We spend the whole day,
Till night by arriving
   Has finished our play.

What then? One and all,
   There's no more to be said,
As we tumbled all day,
   So we tumble to bed.

ANONYMOUS

A Friend

BEATRICE SCHENK DE REGNIERS

Whoever we are,
Whatever we be,
We're friends 'cause I'm me
We're friends 'cause she's she.
(Or because he is he—
Whatever, whatever the case may be.)
A friend
        is a friend
                is a friend!

The artwork for this book is fabric relief. This art form involves many techniques, including appliqué, embroidery, wrapping, dyeing, and soft sculpture. The background fabrics were dyed and then sewn together. Three-dimensional pieces were made from a variety of materials, including covered and stuffed cardboard shapes, wrapped wire, found objects such as seashells and acorn caps, and fabric. Details were embroidered onto the shapes and background, and then the three-dimensional pieces were sewn into place. All stitching was done by hand.

Color transparencies of the artwork were made by Gamma One Conversions and reproduced in full color. The text of the book was set in 14 point Goudy. The book was printed by Barton Press, Inc., and bound by Horowitz/Rae.

Acknowledgments

Grateful acknowledgment is made to the following for permission to use material owned by them. Every reasonable effort has been made to clear the use of the poems in this volume. If notified of any omissions, the publisher will make the necessary corrections in future editions.

"Bursting" by Dorothy Aldis from *All Together*. Copyright 1952 by Dorothy Aldis, copyright © 1980 by Roy E. Porter. Reprinted by permission of G. P. Putnam's Sons.

"A Boy's Place" by Rose Burgunder from *From Summer to Summer*. Copyright © 1965 by Rose Styron. Used by permission of Viking Penguin, a division of Penguin Books USA Inc.

"My Natural Mama" by Lucille Clifton from *Poems for Mothers*. Copyright © 1988 by Lucille Clifton. Published by Holiday House and reprinted by permission of Curtis Brown, Ltd.

"How To Be a Friend" by Pat Lowery Collins. Copyright © 1997 by Pat Lowery Collins. Reprinted by permission of the author.

Last nine lines from "Reply to Someone Who Asked Why the Two of Us Are Such Good Friends" by Beatrice Schenk de Regniers from *A Week in the Life of Best Friends*. Text copyright © 1986 Beatrice Schenk de Regniers. Reprinted with the permission of Atheneum Books for Young Readers, an imprint of Simon & Schuster.

"On Halloween" by Aileen Fisher. Copyright © 1997 by Aileen Fisher. Reprinted by permission of the author.

"two friends" by Nikki Giovanni from *Spin a Soft Black Song*. Copyright © 1985 by Nikki Giovanni. Reprinted by permission of Farrar, Straus & Giroux, Inc.

"Adoption" by Isabel Joshlin Glaser. Copyright © 1997 by Isabel Joshlin Glaser. Used by permission of Marian Reiner for the author.

"Chums" by Arthur Guiterman. Reprinted by permission of Louise H. Sclove.

"Sidewalks" by Patricia Hubbell from *The Tigers Brought Pink Lemonade*. Copyright © 1988 by Patricia Hubbell. Reprinted by permission of Marian Reiner for the author.

"Hope" by Langston Hughes from *Selected Poems*. Copyright 1942 by Alfred A. Knopf, Inc., and renewed 1970 by Arna Bontemps and George Houston Bass. Reprinted by permission of the publisher.

"Teresa's Red Adidas" by Paul B. Janeczko from *This Delicious Day*. Copyright © 1987 by Paul B. Janeczko. Reprinted by permission of the Publisher, Orchard Books, New York.

"Fast Friends" by Monica Kulling. Copyright © 1997 by Monica Kulling. Used by permission of Marian Reiner for the author.

"I Have a Friend" by Karla Kuskin from *Near the Window Tree*. Copyright © 1975 by Karla Kuskin. "Snow" by Karla Kuskin from *Dogs & Dragons, Trees & Dreams*. Copyright © 1980 by Karla Kuskin. Reprinted by permission of HarperCollins Publishers.

"Lemonade Stand" by Myra Cohn Livingston from *Worlds I Know and Other Poems*. Text copyright © 1985 Myra Cohn Livingston. Reprinted with the permission of Margaret K. McElderry Books, an imprint of Simon & Schuster.

"No Girls Allowed" by Jack Prelutsky from *Rolling Harvey down the Hill*. Copyright © 1980 by Jack Prelutsky. By permission of Greenwillow Books, a division of William Morrow & Company, Inc.

"Since Hanna Moved Away" by Judith Viorst from *If I Were in Charge of the World and Other Worries*. Text copyright © 1981 Judith Viorst. Reprinted with the permission of Atheneum Books for Young Readers, an imprint of Simon & Schuster.